JUNIOR ▪ WORLD ▪ BIOGRAPHIES
A JUNIOR *NATIVE AMERICANS OF ACHIEVEMENT* BOOK

Pocahontas

CATHERINE IANNONE

CHELSEA JUNIORS
a division of CHELSEA HOUSE PUBLISHERS

English-language words that are italicized in the text can be found in the glossary at the back of the book.

Chelsea House Publishers

EDITORIAL DIRECTOR Richard Rennert
EXECUTIVE MANAGING EDITOR Karyn Gullen Browne
COPY CHIEF Robin James
PICTURE EDITOR Adrian G. Allen
CREATIVE DIRECTOR Robert Mitchell
ART DIRECTOR Joan Ferrigno
PRODUCTION MANAGER Sallye Scott

JUNIOR WORLD BIOGRAPHIES
SENIOR EDITOR Martin Schwabacher
SERIES DESIGN Marjorie Zaum

Staff for POCAHONTAS

EDITORIAL ASSISTANT Scott D. Briggs
PICTURE RESEARCHER Sandy Jones
COVER ILLUSTRATION Shelley Pritchett

First Printing

1 3 5 7 9 8 6 4 2

Library of Congress Cataloging-in-Publication Data
Iannone, Catherine.
  Pocahontas / Catherine Iannone
    p. cm.—(Junior world biographies)
  Includes bibliographical references and index.
  ISBN 0-7910-2494-6
      0-7910-2497-0 (pbk.)
  1. Pocahontas, d. 1617—Juvenile Literature.
  2. Powhatan women—Biography—Juvenile literature.
  3. Powhatan Indians—Social life and customs—Juvenile literature.
  [1. Pocahontas, d. 1617. 2. Powhatan Indians—Biography. 3.
  Indians of North America—Biography. 4. Women—Biography.]
  I. Title. II. Series.
  E99.P85P5737 1995
  975.5'01'092—dc20   95-7933
  [B]   CIP
                                                                  AC

Contents

Iapassus and his wife convince Pocahontas to visit Captain Samuel Argall's ship. Iapassus was given a copper kettle for helping the English kidnap Pocahontas.

1

Kidnapped

In the spring of 1613, Pocahontas heard that an English ship had sailed into the capital city of the Patawomeke Indians. Pocahontas was living as an honored guest of the Patawomekes. Her father, Powhatan, ruled all the tribes around Chesapeake Bay in present-day Virginia. As the king's daughter, the 18-year-old Pocahontas had come to trade with the Patawomekes and collect *tribute*.

Her host during her visit was Iapassus, one of the town's leaders. Iapassus told Pocahontas that the ship's captain, Samuel Argall, had asked her to visit him. Pocahontas was eager to talk to the English sea captain. He was even more eager to meet with her.

Pocahontas was well known to the English. When they first arrived in her father's territory in 1607 and built a settlement named Jamestown, she was only about 12 years old. She had visited the *colonists* and played with the English children. Powhatan had even sent her to Jamestown on official business.

The English had not seen Pocahontas in several years, but they had not forgotten about her. They knew that as the daughter of the greatest ruler in the entire region, she was a very important person. She had helped them a great deal in the past, and they hoped she could be of use to them again.

Iapassus told Pocahontas that she had been invited to go aboard Argall's ship, the *Treasurer*, and she willingly accepted. Iapassus's wife asked to go along because she had never been on an English ship. Leaving behind her own servants,

Pocahontas went on board the *Treasurer* with Iapassus and his wife and attendants.

Argall and his crew politely welcomed Pocahontas. She and her companions were given a tour of the ship and were served a special meal. Argall then invited his guests to rest before returning to shore.

Because of her royal position, Pocahontas was given a room all to herself. She lay down in the gun room and the door was locked behind her—from the outside. While Pocahontas rested, Iapassus and his wife secretly left the ship.

When they were gone, Argall unlocked the door to Pocahontas's room and announced that she was being taken prisoner. With Pocahontas locked below deck, the *Treasurer* set sail for Jamestown.

Down beneath the ship's deck, Pocahontas had no idea what fate awaited her. Despite the insult of being locked up, however, she must have felt a little curious about seeing Jamestown again. She had very much enjoyed her earlier visits there.

She had tasted strange new foods, such as imported tea, and had learned a few English words. The governor's wife had shown her a book, which had excited her greatly. Pocahontas had made many friends in the English *colony*. Whether she would be treated kindly as she had before, or as a prisoner of war, she did not know.

By kidnapping Powhatan's daughter, Argall was taking a big risk. Relations between the col-

The English founded the colony of Jamestown when Pocahontas was about 12 years old. The young princess enjoyed visiting the town and playing with the English children.

ony and the Native Americans were very bad, and the English feared that a full-scale war could break out at any moment. Although the English had guns and the Indians did not, Powhatan's warriors far outnumbered the residents of Jamestown. Argall was gambling that by taking Pocahontas prisoner, he could prevent Powhatan from attacking the English.

There was no question that the kidnapping would have a huge impact on relations between the Native Americans and the English colonists. The *abduction* of Pocahontas would become the key event in the survival of the colony itself.

*An English colonist's depiction of an Indian village
shows fields of corn, squash, tobacco, and sunflowers.*

2

Before
the English

Pocahontas probably never saw a single white person before the age of 12. Although Spanish and English sailors made occasional visits along the Atlantic coast, contact with Europeans was rare. Before the English started their colony at Jamestown, the Indians in Powhatan's empire lived in a society that was almost completely free from the influence of Europeans.

When the English ships arrived in 1607, there were about 15,000 Indians living under Powhatan's rule. These people belonged to separate tribes, spoke different languages, and differed greatly in appearance. English explorers noted that some were much taller than others and that their customs and lifestyles varied greatly. Over a period of 30 years, Powhatan had united these tribes into one kingdom. He had inherited control over eight of the tribes when his father died. Then, through a series of *conquests,* he had expanded his empire by waging war against all the tribes in the region. By the time the English arrived, he had added about twenty more villages to the eight he had started with. Because these peoples were all ruled by Powhatan, they became known as the Powhatan tribes.

The Powhatan tribes lived in what is now the state of Virginia, mostly along the rivers leading into Chesapeake Bay. This area is known as the Tidewater region because it is where the freshwater rivers meet the salt water of the Atlantic Ocean.

The Tidewater region offered many sources of food. In the rivers and the bay, men gathered

oysters and mussels. They also fished from canoes—some of which were 50 feet long—that were
carved from a single tree trunk. At night, they
sometimes lit fires on their boats to attract fish.
They caught fish in many different ways, using
nets, spears, traps, and lines with bone fishhooks.
They even fished with bows, attaching cords to the
arrows so they could retrieve them.

Bows and arrows were also used to hunt
game such as deer, squirrels, beavers, rabbits, and
wild turkeys. Hunters sometimes disguised themselves as deer so they could get closer to their prey.
They would wear a deerskin, holding up the head
and imitating the animal's movements.

Although some Indian tribes survived solely
by hunting, fishing, and gathering nuts, roots, and
berries, all of the Powhatan tribes were also excellent farmers. Each family had its own garden.
After the men had cleared fields of trees and
bushes, the women dug small holes and planted
seeds in them. As the plants grew, the women
carefully weeded their gardens. Children chased

away animals and birds that tried to eat the growing plants. Some corn was planted in April, some in May, and some in June, so that there would be corn ripening all through the fall.

Children began to learn the skills they would need as adults as soon as they were able.

Boys practiced shooting with small bows to prepare for hunting. Girls learned from their mothers how to tend the gardens, weave baskets, and make clay pots. They also learned how to make clothing from animal skins.

Leather made from deerskin was used to

The Powhatans carved canoes from a single log by burning the wood in the center. When the fire was put out, the burned wood was scraped out with a shell.

make winter clothes such as leggings and moccasins. The wealthier people wore leather robes decorated with shells or beads. Some even had shimmering cloaks made of feathers. Poorer people wore clothing made from leaves and grass that were woven together and tucked into a leather belt.

Except in the coldest weather, most Powhatans wore very little clothing. Often the men and women wore only a breechcloth, which hung from the waist like an apron. Instead of wearing clothing, they preferred to coat their bodies with oil, which helped keep them warm in the winter and cool in the summer. By mixing colored powder into the oil, they could paint their bodies various colors, most often red.

The Powhatans decorated their bodies in many ways. Men sometimes adorned their hair with feathers and a rattle from the tail of a rattlesnake. Some women covered their legs, hands, and faces with tattoos of animals. It was common for both men and women to have three holes in each ear from which they hung beads, chains, and other objects. According to Jamestown colonist John Smith, some men attached live snakes to their ears, and others used as earrings the skins of rats hung by the tail.

Hairstyles differed according to age, sex, and rank. Young girls wore their hair long in the back but cut very short in the front and on the sides. Married women wore their hair the same length all the way around, cut just below the ears. Men kept their hair very long on one side of the head but shaved the other half. That way, their hair could not get tangled in the bowstrings when they shot their bows. Important people who served as priests or magicians shaved the right side of their head but left a tuft of hair above the ear.

Powhatan priests were believed to have magical powers, such as the ability to identify criminals. They were also thought to be able to cure disease and change the weather by communicating with the powerful spirits of the natural world.

Because of their powers and wisdom, the priests served as advisers to the village leader, who was called the *werowance*. There were usually a few priests in each village, but only one werowance. The werowance could be a man or a woman; if it was a woman, she was called a *weronsqua*. When a werowance died, the title went to his brother. If he had no more brothers, his sister would inherit the title. When passed on to the next generation, the title would go not to the werowance's son but to his sister's son.

The werowance in each village was a very powerful figure. If anyone disobeyed him, he could order the offender to be beaten or killed on the spot. All the people in his tribe had to pay him tribute, so he became very wealthy.

Powhatan men could have more than one wife if they were wealthy enough to provide for a larger family. The werowance had the most wives because he was the richest. But any man who was a good enough hunter could have two or more wives.

This portrait of a werowance's wife and daughter gives an idea of how Pocahontas might have appeared as a young girl.

As the ruler of all the werowances in his realm, Powhatan had more wives than anyone else—possibly as many as 100. He probably never had more than 12 at one time, however. After each wife had a child, she was sent back to her village or passed on to another man.

Because of this, Pocahontas had many half brothers and half sisters—children who had the same father but different mothers. According to English observers, Pocahontas was her father's favorite.

Like other children in her tribe, Pocahontas had more than one name. Her clan name, which was used only within her family, was Matoaka, which meant "playful" or "frolicsome." The name she used in public, Pocahontas, meant "mischievous" or "frisky." Although little is known of her early years, it is clear from the names that were chosen for her that she was a friendly, spirited child.

There is no record of her mother, probably because Pocahontas was raised in her father's household. As a daughter of not only a werowance but of the supreme king of all the werowances, she had a very privileged childhood. While most Powhatan girls had to help their mothers collect wood, cook, and work in the garden, Pocahontas probably had more time to swim in the rivers and play in the forest. However, she also learned to behave as a royal princess and fulfill the important functions of tribal leaders. By sitting next to her father during meetings and ceremonies, she learned to act in a dignified manner that would command respect.

The combination of Pocahontas's outgoing nature and her royal manner made her well suited to represent her father on official trips to other villages. These qualities became even more important after the arrival of the English.

The locations of the Tidewater tribes and the first English settlements in Virginia in the 17th century.

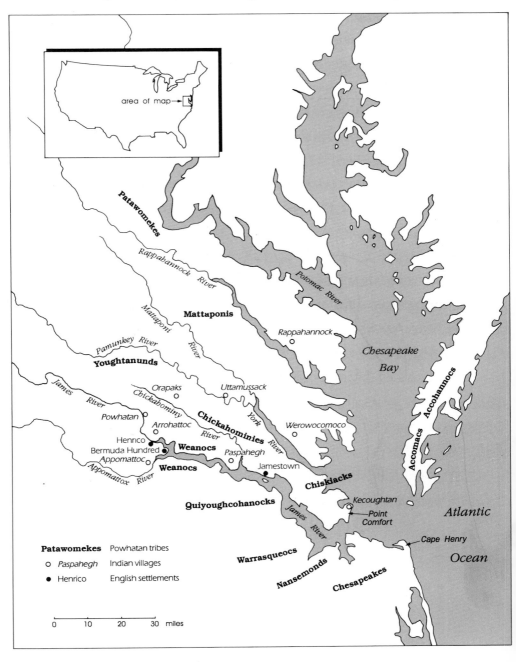

area of map→

Patawomekes

Rappahannock River

Potomac River

Mattaponis

Mattaponi River

Rappahannock
○

Pamunkey River

Chesapeake
Bay

Youghtanunds

Orapaks
○

Uttamussack

Chickahominies

Chickahominy

James River

Powhatan
○

Arrohattoc
○

York River

Werowocomoco
○

Accohannocs

Henrico ●
Bermuda Hundred ●
Appomattoc ○

Weanocs

Paspahegh
○

Accomacs

Appomattox River

Weanocs

Jamestown ●

Chiskiacks

Quiyoughcohanocks

James River

Kecoughtan
○
—Point
Comfort

Atlantic

Cape Henry

Ocean

Patawomekes   Powhatan tribes
○ *Paspahegh*   Indian villages
● Henrico   English settlements

Warrasqueocs

Nansemonds

Chesapeakes

0   10   20   30   miles

3

Jamestown

At the time the English built the Jamestown colony, the country with the biggest presence in the Americas was Spain. Spanish explorers had conquered Native American peoples such as the Aztecs in Mexico and the Incas in South America. The Spanish had also sent explorers and traders to what would become the United States. Spanish ships had carried home tons of gold and silver stolen from American Indians.

As a lesser sea power, the English had to content themselves with trying to rob the Spanish ships as they returned. Pirates such as Sir Francis Drake stole much of the wealth the Spanish had looted from the newly discovered continent.

Near the end of the 16th century, the balance of naval power began to shift toward the English. In 1588, the king of Spain sent his powerful navy to crush the British once and for all. However, in a shocking turnabout, the English navy defeated the Spanish. No longer afraid of the Spanish navy, the English vowed to compete with Spain in America.

The English made several attempts to build outposts in America, including one on Roanoke Island in present-day North Carolina, but all of them failed. In April 1605, King James granted permission to the Virginia Company of London to establish two new colonies. One was North Virginia, which would later be called New England. It was settled by hardworking Puritans seeking religious freedom. The other colony, South Virginia, was made up mostly of noblemen without land and people the English wanted to get rid of, such as poor people and criminals. This group headed for the Tidewater area of modern-day Virginia.

On April 26, 1607, three ships—the *Susan Constant,* the *Godspeed,* and the *Discovery*—arrived in Chesapeake Bay. Sixteen of the 120 passengers had died during the difficult 18-week journey. Although the survivors were eager to reach land, they waited until dark to send a group ashore.

Despite their precautions, they were spotted by a group of Indians. One of the noblemen, George Percy, wrote of the encounter: "There came the Savages creeping upon all foure, from the Hills, like Beares; with their Bowes in their mouthes [they] charged us." The Indians ran away, however, when the English fired a musket at them. They had never seen or heard a gun before and were frightened by the sound of the explosion.

Near the mouth of Chesapeake Bay, the English found a large river, which they named the James River. Percy was very impressed with the beauty of the area. He described the many branches of the river "flowing through the Woods with great plentie of fish of all kindes," and he wrote admiringly of the "many sweet and delicate flowres" on their shores.

Exploring parties traveled up the James River in small boats, looking for a place to settle. They chose a spot near where the Chickahominy River joins the James River. They did not see any people there, so they assumed the land was theirs for the taking. They did not know that they were actually right in the middle of Powhatan's empire.

The colonists had their second encounter with the Indians while exploring near the mouth

When the English landed in Powhatan's territory, most of the Indians had never seen Europeans.

of the James River, at a place they named Point Comfort. A small group led by Christopher Newport, the captain of the *Susan Constant*, saw four Indians on shore and rowed over to them. Newport laid his hand over his heart to show he came in peace. The Indians understood and responded by laying down their bows and arrows.

The Indians brought the Englishmen to their village, Kecoughtan, to meet their werowance, whose name was Pochins. He was one of Powhatan's sons (and thus Pocahontas's half brother). Pochins offered them a feast, and they smoked a peace pipe together. On May 4, another group met the werowance of Paspahegh, a village about 10 miles from Jamestown.

Several weeks later, the werowance of Paspahegh came to visit Jamestown. He brought about 100 warriors with him, which made the colonists uneasy. The Indians offered the meat of a large deer as a gift and suggested the colonists put down their weapons. The English refused, fearing a trick. The two groups were very suspicious of each other, and a fight nearly broke out when an Indian tried to take a hatchet from an Englishman. The Paspahegh werowance became so angry that he ordered his party to depart.

Eight days later, the Paspahegh Indians launched a brief attack on Jamestown. Other groups made raids on the colony, but some remained friendly and wanted to trade with the newcomers. Each village acted differently, so the colonists never knew what to expect.

Because they were sometimes attacked while walking in the forest, the settlers began to wear their heavy metal armor whenever they went outside the fort. This made hunting extremely difficult. The English still had no farms or gardens, and were either too afraid or too lazy to hunt and fish. Many of the colonists were *aristocrats* and expected others to do all the work. By early summer, they were already running out of food, and on June 22, Captain Newport set sail for England to bring back supplies.

The only man on Jamestown's ruling council who was not a nobleman was John Smith. He was born a commoner, and his parents had died by the time he was 15 years old. Though he was only 27 when he arrived in Virginia, he had fought in several wars and had made his way across Europe, getting captured and escaping more than once.

Smith had nothing but scorn for the lazy noblemen. In fact, he had been imprisoned on the voyage to America for refusing to obey the trip's leaders. In Virginia, he took action to acquire food for the settlers. He was not at all reluctant to clash with the Indians, and he led parties to Indian villages to trade beads and other trinkets for baskets of corn.

On one trip up the Chickahominy River, the river became too narrow for Smith to continue by boat. Taking an Indian guide with him, he left his party by the boat and went off to explore the forest.

Suddenly, a group of Indians surprised him. One shot him in the leg with an arrow. Smith fired his gun to keep them at a distance. While backing away, however, he fell into the water and was captured.

The attackers took him to their werowance, who was Powhatan's brother Opechancanough. The quick-thinking Smith took a compass from his pocket and gave it to Opechancanough. The Indians had never seen a compass before, so they thought it was a magical object. Thinking Smith had special powers, Opechancanough decided to bring him to see Powhatan himself.

In this illustration from John Smith's Generall Historie of Virginia, *Smith battles the Pamunkey Indians in a swamp and is captured when he falls into the water.*

No European had ever before seen the mighty Powhatan. Smith was greatly impressed to find the king's village, Werowocomoco, to be a thriving town. While the English were struggling to survive in Jamestown, Powhatan was living in splendor, surrounded by large fields of corn, beans, and pumpkins.

Smith was received in Powhatan's long-house, an imposing structure about 60 feet long. He was dazzled by Powhatan's regal manner and the clothing and decorations of his wives and attendants. Powhatan provided a lavish feast. While they ate, he consulted with the other Indians about what to do with Smith.

Finally, Powhatan ordered his guards to place two large stone blocks before him. Smith was then forced to kneel and lay his head on the blocks. Powhatan had apparently decided what to do with the intruder. His men raised their clubs above their heads, preparing to smash open Smith's head.

In The Generall Historie of Virginia, *Pocahontas was portrayed saving Smith's life after Powhatan had ordered his execution.*

King Powhatan comands C:Smith to be slayne,
daughter Pokahontas beggs his life his thankfulln
and how he subiected 39 of their kings. reade y histor

4

The Young Ambassador

Smith was preparing to take his last breath when he felt another body flung across his own. Turning his head as far as he could, he saw that his savior was the young Pocahontas. Just before the clubs fell on both of them, Powhatan ordered a halt to the execution.

Years later, Smith described this episode in his book *The Generall Historie of Virginia, New England, and the Summer Isles.* The story of Smith's rescue by Pocahontas has become an

American legend. And as with most legends, it is difficult to know how much of the story is true.

Smith did not write about the incident until many years after it was supposed to have happened. This has led some scholars to believe that Smith made up the story after Pocahontas became famous. Perhaps he wanted to increase his own fame by associating himself with Pocahontas. It is also possible that he was trying to claim that Pocahontas was the one noble Indian among a tribe of violent savages. By the time his *Generall Historie* was published in 1624, the English were trying to take over the Powhatans' territory. The English often tried to justify taking the Indians' land by portraying them as ignorant brutes who deserved to be conquered.

According to other historians, Smith actually believed that Pocahontas saved him from execution, when she may in fact have been performing a ritual adoption of Smith. Perhaps the adoption ceremony included a fake execution to symbolize the end of one life and the beginning of a new one as a member of the tribe. In this case, Pocahontas may have placed her body over his to symbolize his rebirth.

Whether or not Powhatan adopted Smith, he did treat the English differently after Smith's *captivity.* Powhatan expected the English to be his *subjects,* as were the other tribes in the Powhatan Confederacy. He offered to feed and protect the English in exchange for English arms and metal tools. Captain Smith accepted the offer, although he had no intention of giving the Indians any weapons. He knew that those weapons might someday be used against the English.

Shortly after Smith returned to Jamestown, Captain Newport arrived with nearly 100 new settlers from England. The residents of Jamestown, who were in danger of going hungry over the winter, were relieved that Newport had also brought a supply of food. However, tragedy struck the colony five days later. On January 7, 1608, a fire swept through the town. Among the many buildings left in ashes was the storehouse that held the town's food. Once again, the colonists were faced with starvation.

Soon after the fire, a group of Powhatans arrived at Jamestown carrying cornbread, meat, and fish. Smith would later claim that Pocahontas had brought the food against her father's wishes. Once again, he wanted his fellow Englishmen to think that Pocahontas was the only Indian who helped the colony. But it was Powhatan who sent the provisions. Powhatan was treating the English as he would treat any of his subjects—by feeding them in time of need. He was upholding the agreement he had made with Smith in December. Throughout January and February, the people of Jamestown looked on in wonder as Indian messengers arrived bearing more and more food.

During this time, Powhatan invited the English to visit him. At the end of February, Smith and Newport and about 40 colonists sailed to Werowocomoco to visit the great chief. Smith presented Powhatan with gifts from England, including a red woolen suit, a hat, and a white greyhound. Powhatan feasted the colonists and gave them large amounts of bread to bring home.

The visit went well until Powhatan asked the English to put down their weapons, as all of his subjects did in his presence. The English refused, fearing that the Indians would attack them or steal their weapons. From the Indians' viewpoint, Smith was breaking his promise to Powhatan. But Smith pacified the chief by promising to bring two enemy tribes into Powhatan's empire. Powhatan was satisfied with this response and still considered the colonists to be his subjects.

Captain John Smith's trading expeditions may have saved Jamestown from starvation, but his brash, bold, and sometimes violent behavior made him lose favor with the colony's leaders.

The following day, Captain Newport presented Powhatan with a boy named Thomas Savage, who would live with the Powhatans and learn their language. The Indians in turn sent a boy named Namontack to live with the English.

After the visit to Werowocomoco, relations between the English and the Powhatans worsened. The English did not appreciate Powhatan's attempts to bring them into his empire, and the Indians were offended that the colonists would not lay down their guns.

Powhatan stopped protecting the English, and his subjects soon began launching minor attacks and stealing tools from Jamestown. The colonists took several men hostage in order to force the Indians to return the tools. The Powhatans tried to get the hostages released by capturing Englishmen, but this only increased hostilities. The Powhatan captives were finally freed in May 1608, when Pocahontas went to Jamestown bearing a gift of corn and a personal request from her father.

After this first visit, Pocahontas began spending a lot of time in Jamestown. She enjoyed playing with the English boys. They taught her to turn cartwheels, and she often outdid them in running races and jumping competitions.

Despite Pocahontas's friendly relations with the English, the Powhatans were growing more suspicious of the colonists. The English were exploring the region and contacting tribes on the border of Powhatan's territory. The chief worried that the English were trying to turn local tribes against him. And Smith, who was elected president of Jamestown, continued to *intimidate* the Indians with his heavy-handed *negotiating*.

Powhatan's anger at the British increased after Captain Newport's return to the colony on October 8, 1608. King James had ordered Newport to invite Powhatan to Jamestown and crown him emperor. This *coronation* was a way of tricking Powhatan into becoming a subject of King James. If he let himself be crowned by the king, it would mean that he accepted the king's rule. The

English assumed that Powhatan was too naive to realize the meaning of the ceremony.

Powhatan, however, had a sophisticated understanding of politics. He knew that the English were trying to undermine his power. The chief was insulted that the English expected him to travel to Jamestown for the coronation. In Powhatan's empire, as in Europe, a person who had business with the king had to go see the king. Powhatan told Smith:

> If your King have sent me presents, I also am a King, and this is my land. . . . Your father [Captain Newport] is to come to me, not I to him, nor yet to your Fort, neither will I bite at such a bait.

Smith and Newport were disappointed with this response. Holding the ceremony at Werowocomoco would reduce the dignity of the occasion. But they had to follow their king's orders and crown Powhatan, even if it meant doing it on his terms.

Powhatan only grew more irritated during his coronation. King James had specifically ordered that Powhatan kneel as a sign of *submission* to the English king. Powhatan, however, refused to kneel. Smith and Newport were determined to carry out the king's orders, so they had someone push down on Powhatan's shoulders while they put the crown on his head.

Following this ridiculous ceremony, Powhatan's patience with the English was running low. He knew that they were trying to take over his dominion, and he would no longer assist them by providing food. The summer of 1608 had been dry, and both the colonists and the Indians had had poor harvests. The Indians had little food to spare, and Powhatan had told his people not to trade with the English. When the English found that the Indians would not trade with them, they took what they wanted by force.

In December, Powhatan offered to trade corn to the English, but fighting erupted shortly after the English arrived in Werowocomoco. After this skirmish, Powhatan decided to leave the village and move farther away from the English. From this point on, he would divide his time between the towns of Orapax and Rassawrack.

The colonists then sailed up the Pamunkey River to acquire provisions from Powhatan's

King James ordered the colonists to crown Powhatan emperor. Sensing that the English were only trying to make him accept the king's authority, Powhatan refused to kneel during the ceremony.

brother Opechancanough, the werowance of the Pamunkey Indians. The Pamunkeys were willing to trade, but tensions arose between the two groups. The Indians attacked the English. Smith then forced the Pamunkeys to sell their corn by taking hold of Opechancanough and putting a gun to his chest. The werowance was outraged at this treatment. The English paid a high price for their corn by angering the man who would one day rule the Powhatan Confederacy.

Pocahontas's visits to Jamestown ended around this time. Naturally, Powhatan did not want his daughter visiting people who were quickly becoming his enemies. But the colonists probably would have stopped seeing Pocahontas even if their relations with her father had remained friendly. Pocahontas was now 13 years old, a time of major changes for Powhatan girls. It was no longer appropriate for her to go to Jamestown on her own and play with the English boys. Pocahontas was expected to start acting like an adult and thinking about marriage.

The Powhatans were skilled in growing and gathering food in the rich Tidewater region. The English, however, were unable to feed themselves during their first years in Virginia.

5

The Starving Time

While Pocahontas stayed away from Jamestown, relations between the English and the Powhatans deteriorated further. Throughout the early months of 1609, the Indians launched many attacks on Jamestown. Smith worked hard to strengthen the colony. He enlarged the fort and cleared more land for farming. He was a stern leader and he demanded discipline and hard work from all the colonists, even the noblemen. Under his leadership, the colony was finally becoming productive and growing stronger. However, his harsh rule made him unpopular with many settlers, especially the aristocrats.

In July 1609, Captain Samuel Argall arrived from England with important news. The Virginia Company of London had sent a fleet of ships, called the Third Relief Supply. The ships were due to arrive in Jamestown any day, carrying 600 new settlers and supplies for the colony. Smith was relieved by the news. With the new settlers, the colony would be better able to defend itself against Indian raids.

But Smith's relief quickly turned to anger when he heard the rest of Argall's news. A new governor had been placed in charge of Virginia. Upon hearing this, Smith resigned from the presidency. After all the work he had put into improving the colony, he would not take orders from someone who had never even set foot in Virginia. He decided to leave Jamestown and live on his own.

Smith obtained land from Parahunt, Poca-hontas's half brother. But Smith never had a chance to build his new house. On his way back to Jamestown, a bag of gunpowder that he was carrying exploded. Smith was so badly injured that he decided to give up on Virginia and return to England. Many colonists blamed Smith for the poor conditions in Jamestown, and they were happy to see him go. On October 1, 1609, Smith left for England. He would never see Virginia again.

Soon after Smith left Virginia, Powhatan was told that the captain had died. The English probably said this to make the chief realize that he would not be dealing with Smith again. But Powhatan did not want to deal with anyone else. He had often been angered by Smith's brash be-havior, but he respected Smith more than any other Englishman. With Smith gone, the Indians began raiding the colony more frequently.

The English realized that they were in for

another tough winter, and this time they could not count on any assistance from the Indians. The Third Relief Supply had not arrived in July, as Argall had said it would. A powerful hurricane had thrown the ships off course. In September 1609, seven of the ships finally arrived at Jamestown. The passengers were exhausted from the long voyage, and during the extra months they spent at sea, they had used up many of the provisions that they were bringing to the colony. Now winter was approaching and the colony had more settlers to feed from its decreasing stores.

Just as the supply of food was getting dangerously low, the colonists received an invitation from Powhatan. He was offering to trade corn, but the English were suspicious. Powhatan had grown increasingly hostile toward the colonists. It seemed strange that he would want to help them, but they were too hungry to turn down his invitation.

When 62 Englishmen arrived in Orapax in November 1609, they found that their suspicions of Powhatan were justified. The Indians attacked, killing 60 men. A boy named Samuell was taken prisoner, and only one man made it back to Jamestown. When the other colonists heard about the massacre, they knew that they were completely on their own. Winter was almost upon them and they had almost no food to get them through it.

Pocahontas was angered by her father's attack on the English. Soon after the massacre, she moved 90 miles north of her father's home to live with the Patawomekes, who belonged to the Powhatan Confederacy. Officially, Pocahontas was living with them as a representative of her father. The only thing that the colonists heard about her during this time was a rumor that she had married a Patawomeke named Kocoum. No one is sure that the marriage actually took place.

For the residents of Jamestown, the winter of 1609–10 would come to be known as the "starving time." Hunger and disease ravaged the colony. Indians attacked any Englishman they found, so the colonists were virtually held captive within their own fort. The desperate colonists resorted to eating "dogs Catts Ratts and myce." One man was executed for murdering and eating his wife. Of the 490 colonists living in Jamestown, only 60 survived the winter.

Help did not arrive until May, when the remainder of the Third Relief Supply arrived. One ship, the *Sea Venture,* had become separated from the other ships during the hurricane. Among the *Sea Venture*'s passengers was Sir Thomas Gates, the new deputy governor of Virginia. The colonists had assumed that the ship had sunk. It had actually been blown off course and landed on Bermuda. The passengers lived on Bermuda for 10 months. From the wreckage of the *Sea Venture* they built two new ships, the *Deliverance* and the *Patience*.

When the ships arrived in Jamestown on May 23, 1610, the passengers were expecting to find a thriving colony. Their hearts sank at the pitiful condition of Jamestown. The fort was falling apart. Many buildings had been torn down and used as firewood because the colonists had been too scared to leave the fort in search of wood. The few remaining colonists were sick and starving.

Sir Thomas Gates saw no way to save the colony. He ordered the colonists to abandon Virginia and return to England. On June 7, 1610, the *Deliverance* and the *Patience* set sail down the James River. Powhatan had succeeded in driving the English from his kingdom.

But an amazing coincidence prevented the desertion of Jamestown. As the ships approached the Atlantic Ocean, the crew saw three English ships on the horizon. The ships carried 150 new settlers, including the new governor of the colony, Lord De La Warr. The governor had great plans for Virginia and he was not willing to give up on the colony. He declared that the timing of his arrival was a sign from God that the English should carry on. Under his command, the colonists returned to Jamestown.

Lord De La Warr blamed Jamestown's problems on the laziness of its citizens. He revived the colony by governing it in much the same way that John Smith had. He established a work schedule and supervised the rebuilding of the fort. He also ordered the clearing of more land so that the town could grow enough crops to feed itself.

De La Warr's firm leadership succeeded in restoring the colony, but it did not improve relations with the Indians. De La Warr tried to force Powhatan to trade by threatening him. Of course, Powhatan had no reason to fear the English. They had not even shown the ability to survive without the help of the Indians. He warned the English either to leave his kingdom or to stay inside their fort.

De La Warr wanted to prove that his threats were real. In August 1610, he ordered an attack on the town of Paspahegh. The English reported killing about 70 people and setting fire to the town. They even captured and killed the wife and children of the werowance. The killing of women and children, especially the family of a werowance, was a grave offense among the Powhatans. After this atrocious act, Powhatan refused to communicate with the English and he ordered his people to increase their attacks.

Pocahontas was finally seen again during this time of tension. In the early fall of 1610, Pocahontas and Pasptanze (the werowance of the Patawomekes) visited Powhatan at Rassawrack. Three English boys were living with Powhatan. Thomas Savage and Henry Spelman had been sent by the English to learn the Powhatan language and act as interpreters. The third boy, who is known only by the name Samuell, had been captured during the massacre of 1609.

Spelman later wrote that he was anxious to return to Jamestown. The hostility between the English and the Powhatans had put him in an uncomfortable situation. When Powhatan had planned the massacre in 1609, he had sent Spelman to Jamestown to invite the colonists to Werowocomoco. Although Spelman, Savage, and Samuell were treated well by Powhatan, they did not want to continue living with the enemy of their countrymen. Spelman later wrote that Pasptanze "shewed such kindness to Savage, Samuell, and myself, as we determine to goe away with him."

When Pocahontas and Pasptanze left Rassawrack, the three boys secretly followed them. However, Savage had second thoughts. He had lived with Powhatan for over two years, and the chief had treated him very well. According to Spelman, when the boys were about a mile from Rassawrack, Savage turned back and told Powhatan about the escape. Powhatan was furious and sent a party of warriors after the runaways. The Indians found the boys and ordered them to return. Instead, Spelman and Samuell tried to flee. One warrior caught Samuell and killed him. The horrified Spelman raced into the woods and escaped.

Sir Thomas Dale was a demanding leader who greatly strengthened the Virginia colony.

Pocahontas and Pasptanze allowed Spelman to stay with the Patawomekes and protected him from Powhatan. Spelman later said that Pocahontas treated him very kindly. The story of Pocahontas's charity toward Spelman soon reached England. The colonists were anxious to prove that their situation was not hopeless. They hoped that stories of the kindhearted Indian princess would convince the Virginia Company of London that at least some of the Indians were friendly with the English. This would encourage the company to invest more money in the colony and to send more settlers.

Soon after Spelman's arrival among the Patawomekes, another Englishman encountered Pocahontas. In September 1610, Captain Argall lost his way and ended up on the Potomac River, where he met the Patawomekes. He was relieved to find that Pasptanze was willing to trade with him in spite of Powhatan's ban on trade. The captain was also happy to find Henry Spelman alive and well. But he was most excited to learn that Pocahontas was living there. He thought that she might be useful in dealing with Powhatan.

In March 1611, De La Warr left Virginia because of poor health. Sir Thomas Dale, the new deputy governor, arrived in May. Dale was even more demanding than De La Warr. Under his leadership the colony was soon thriving and expanding. But the English knew that their success would be limited as long as the war with Powhatan continued.

There was one person, however, who they believed could be the key to holding off the mighty Powhatan, and now they knew where she was. Although it was risky, they decided to put their daring plan to kidnap Pocahontas into action.

The baptism of Pocahontas gave the English
hope that they could live in peace with the Indians.

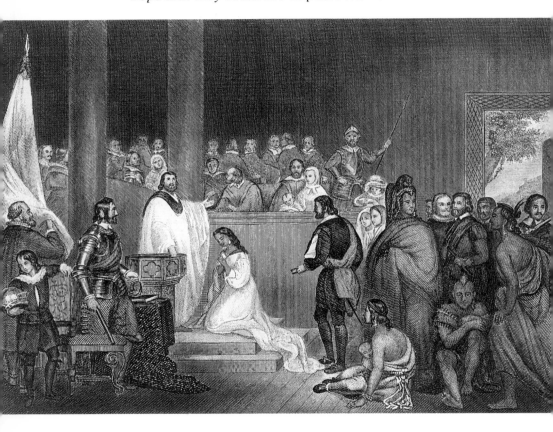

CHAPTER

6

To England

In April 1613, Captain Argall traveled to Pasp-tanze's village and met with the werowance's younger brother, Iapassus. Argall warned that if the Patawomekes did not hand over Pocahontas, the English would wage war on them. The Pata-womekes discussed the matter for several hours and decided that they did not want to risk war with the English. Iapassus and his wife agreed to assist Argall in kidnapping Pocahontas and helped lure her aboard the English ship.

Pocahontas was very angry to discover that she had been betrayed by both the English and the Patawomekes. When she arrived in Jamestown, she showed none of the joy and curiosity she had displayed on her earlier visits. Now, surrounded by guards, she walked slowly with her eyes to the ground.

A messenger was sent to inform Powhatan that his daughter was being held hostage. She would be released only if Powhatan returned all the Englishmen he had captured as well as the tools and weapons his people had stolen. But as much as Powhatan loved his daughter, he was not willing to make peace with the English.

When the colonists realized that Powhatan would not ransom his daughter, they decided to use her for another purpose. One of the original goals of the Virginia colony was to *convert* the Indians to Christianity. Leaders of the Virginia Company had even suggested kidnapping young Indians so that they could live among the English and learn their religion. Pocahontas would be the first Powhatan Indian to be educated in Christianity and in the manners and customs of the English.

Pocahontas lived on the farm of the Reverend Alexander Whitaker, who instructed her in the beliefs of Christianity. She had to adapt to an entirely new way of life. As a young girl, she had enjoyed learning about English culture, but now, at age 18, she was being forced to adopt these ways and become an English lady.

The first step in Pocahontas's transformation was shedding her Indian clothing. Her deerskin skirt was replaced with a tight-fitting corset, a long-sleeved blouse, and a skirt that reached her ankles. She was also taught to walk like a lady, with her head bowed modestly.

Alexander Whitaker had been anxious to convert the Indians, and Pocahontas proved to be an excellent student. With her keen intelligence and intense curiosity, she quickly learned to speak English and memorized many prayers.

While living at Whitaker's house, Pocahontas met a man named John Rolfe. Rolfe had arrived at Jamestown in 1610, having sailed from England aboard the *Sea Venture*. During the 10 months the passengers spent on Bermuda, Rolfe's wife had given birth to a daughter. Before they made it to Jamestown, however, both his wife and their baby died.

In Virginia, Rolfe became a successful tobacco farmer. He probably met Pocahontas at one of Whitaker's services. The two became fast friends, and soon they fell in love.

Rolfe was a devout Christian, and he feared that it would be improper to marry someone who had been born a non-Christian. He wrote a letter to Sir Dale explaining his deep love for Pocahontas. He explained his fears and asked Dale for advice. Dale thought that the marriage was a wonderful idea. The marriage of an Englishman to an Indian princess might mean the end of hostilities with the Powhatans.

In March 1614, Dale, Rolfe, Pocahontas, and 150 colonists went to see Powhatan and tell him about the planned wedding. When the English arrived, Powhatan sent two of his sons to the ship to see Pocahontas. The princess told her half brothers that the English were treating her well and that she wished to continue living with them. Rolfe then sent a message to Powhatan telling him of his desire to marry Pocahontas.

To the surprise of the English, Powhatan sent word that not only did he approve of the wedding, but he also wanted to make peace with the English. Powhatan was now about 80 years old, and he was tired of fighting.

On April 5, 1614, Pocahontas and John Rolfe were married. Powhatan would not go to Jamestown to attend the wedding, but he sent one of Pocahontas's uncles and two of her brothers. As a wedding gift, Powhatan gave the couple a piece of land on the shore of the James River.

Before her wedding, Pocahontas had been baptized a Christian and renamed Rebecca. Sir Thomas Dale was excited about Pocahontas's conversion and marriage. It would prove to the Virginia Company that the colony was succeeding in spreading English civilization to North America. Pocahontas gave the English hope that they would be able to live in harmony with the Indians and teach them English customs and religion.

Dale hoped to further improve relations with Powhatan by marrying his youngest daughter. Dale sent a representative, Ralph Hamor, to make the proposal to the chief. Powhatan told Hamor that his daughter was already due to marry a neighboring werowance. Then, after asking about Pocahontas and hearing that she was happy, he told Hamor to bring a message to Dale: "There have been too many of his men and mine slaine, and by my occasion there shall never be more . . . for I am now olde and would gladly end my daies in peace."

Thus Pocahontas's marriage to John Rolfe led to a period that would later be called the Peace of Pocahontas. There were still occasional skirmishes, but for the next eight years, relations between the English and the Powhatans were generally friendly.

Now that the English had established peace with the Indians, there was one more obstacle to expanding the colony. King James was not interested in spending money on colonies in the Americas. The Virginia Company of London realized that it would have to convince others to invest in the colony. Dale suggested sending Pocahontas to England to show what progress they were making with the Indians. He believed that the dignified and intelligent Pocahontas, who could now speak English well, would inspire people to invest in the colony.

In the spring of 1616, when she was about 21 years old, Pocahontas sailed for England with her husband and their son, Thomas, who had been born the previous year. About a dozen other Powhatan men and women also made the trip. Pocahontas's fame had already spread to England, and her arrival caused an immediate sensation. The English were impressed by her regal demeanor. They were also fascinated by the exotic appearance of her Indian companions.

One tribesman, Tomocomo, was wearing a short leather breechcloth decorated with the head and tail of an animal. He had painted his face and body and had tied back his hair with a stuffed snake and the skin of a weasel. Powhatan had instructed Tomocomo to count all the people in England. Tomocomo was overwhelmed by the number of people he saw, and he gave up trying to count them soon after he arrived. He later told Powhatan that the English numbered as many "as the stars in the sky, the sand on the English beaches, or the leaves on the trees."

Powhatan also told Tomocomo to find John Smith, for the chief did not believe that he had actually died. Shortly after her arrival, Pocahontas heard that Smith was indeed alive and in England. She was angry that the English had lied about his death. During her stay in England, she grew even angrier when Smith neglected to visit her.

Pocahontas and her companions were stunned by the size of London and by its impressive sights. They saw London Bridge, Westminster

Abbey, and St. Paul's Cathedral. But the highlight of Pocahontas's trip was a meeting with Queen Anne, the wife of King James. To commemorate the event, the Virginia Company commissioned an official portrait of Pocahontas. In the painting, she looks like a true English noblewoman, wearing a velvet dress with a wide lace collar.

During her stay in England, Pocahontas attended numerous social events and met the elite of English society. The bishop of London threw a

This portrait of Pocahontas and her son, Thomas, once hung in Heacham Hall, the ancestral home of John Rolfe.

party in her honor. Samuel Purchas, one of the party guests, later wrote that Pocahontas "carried herself as a Daughter of a King, and was accordingly respected not only by the great Virginia Company . . . but [by many] persons of Honour."

After several weeks of socializing with the English aristocracy, Pocahontas began to feel ill. The damp, smoke-filled air of London was blamed for her illness, so the Rolfes went to the town of Brentford, a short distance away.

While Pocahontas was recuperating, she finally received a visit from John Smith. Smith later wrote that upon his arrival, "without any word, she turned about, obscured her face, as not seeming well contented." Pocahontas was obviously overwhelmed with emotion at seeing Smith, whom she had not seen for eight years. She had to be alone for several hours before she could bring herself to talk to him.

When she began to speak, she reminded Smith of the help her family had given him and criticized him for breaking the agreements he had made with her father. "You did promise Powhatan what was yours should bee his, and he the like to you; you called him father being in his land a stranger, and by the same reason so must I doe you." Although she was disappointed that Smith had not kept his word, Pocahontas continued, "I tell you then I will, and you shall call mee childe, and so I will bee for ever and ever your Countrieman." She went on to reproach Smith, "They did tell us alwaies you were dead, and I knew no other till I came to Plimoth; yet Powhatan did command [Tomocomo] to seeke you, and know the truth, because your Countriemen will lie much." After this conversation, Smith left Brentford, never to see Pocahontas again.

In March 1617, the Rolfes prepared to return to Virginia. Pocahontas's seven-month stay in England had succeeded in raising a good deal of money for the colony and convincing more people to settle in America. Now she and her family were eager to return home. However, Pocahontas would never again see her homeland.

The 1622 massacre of 330 English colonists ended the era of peace established by Pocahontas's marriage.

As her ship sailed down the Thames River toward the Atlantic Ocean, Pocahontas's condition grew worse. Samuel Argall, who was captaining the ship, gave orders to dock at the town of Gravesend, and Pocahontas was carried to a nearby inn. John Rolfe realized that his wife was dying. Pocahontas tried to comfort her grief-stricken husband, saying, "all must die. 'Tis enough that the child liveth." A short time later, Pocahontas died. She was given a funeral and buried at St. George's Parish Church.

When John Rolfe sailed for Virginia, he also had to leave his son behind. Thomas was too ill to make the trip. He remained in England, where he was raised by John Rolfe's brother.

Upon his return to Virginia, Rolfe sent a message to Powhatan informing him of the death of Pocahontas. Soon after, Powhatan passed his supreme power to his brothers Opitchapan and Opechancanough. About a year later, in April 1618, Powhatan died.

The new rulers of the Powhatans assured the English that they would continue to respect Powhatan's peace. But Opechancanough was a warlike leader and he resented English attempts to take over the Powhatans' territory and convert the Indians. On March 22, 1622, Opechancanough ordered the Powhatans to attack all English colonists. By the end of the day, 330 English people—more than one-quarter of the colony's population—had been killed. John Rolfe also died around this time, but historians do not know if he was killed in the massacre or if he died of some other cause.

After the massacre, the English were determined to drive the Indians from Virginia. The colonists now wanted to convince people in England that the colony's mission should not be to convert and civilize the Indians but to remove them from their land. The colonists had previously sent Pocahontas to England as an example of the nobility of the Indians and the possibility of peace between the Powhatans and the English. Now the colonists depicted the Indians as violent, unintelligent savages.

John Smith published his *Generall Historie of Virginia* two years after the massacre. Smith also portrayed the Indians, including Powhatan himself, as barbarians. He claimed that only one Indian was responsible for helping the struggling colony—Pocahontas. This is why Smith's stories are not accepted as complete truth: any help received from Powhatan or his werowances was credited to Pocahontas.

Although Pocahontas's life is shrouded in legend, there is no doubt that she played an important role in the success of the Jamestown colony. With her marriage and her conversion to Christianity, she forged the first important link between her own people and the English. Today she is a symbol of the possibility for unity between people of vastly different backgrounds.

In 1635, Pocahontas's 20-year-old son, Thomas Rolfe, returned to Virginia from England. His grandfather, Powhatan, had left him thousands of acres of land with which Rolfe became a successful tobacco farmer. He married and raised a family, and his descendants are among the most distinguished families of Virginia. They are proud to trace their ancestry back to the legendary Powhatan peacemaker, Pocahontas.

Further Reading

Fradin, Dennis B. *The Virginia Colony*. Chicago:
Children's Press, 1986.

Fritz, Jean. *The Double Life of Pocahontas*. New York:
Putnam, 1983.

Graves, Charles P. *John Smith*. New York: Chelsea
House, 1991.

Holler, Anne. *Pocahontas: Powhatan Peacemaker*.
New York: Chelsea House, 1993.

McDaniel, Melissa. *The Powhatan Indians*. New York:
Chelsea House, 1995.

Glossary

abduction   a kidnapping

aristocrat   a member of the upper class in a society ruled by a monarch

captivity   the state of being held prisoner

colonist   a person who lives in a colony

colony   a settlement that a country establishes in a distant land

conquest   the defeat of a group of people through warfare

convert   to cause another person to give up his religion and accept a new one; also, to choose to change one's own religion

coronation   a ceremony in which a person is made a king or queen

intimidate   to frighten someone in order to control his actions

negotiating   working out an agreement

subject   someone under the rule of a monarch

submission   the act of placing oneself under the control of another

tribute   a payment made to a ruler by his subjects

werowance   the leader of a Powhatan village

Chronology

c. 1595	Pocahontas is born in what is now Virginia.
April 26, 1607	English settlers arrive in Powhatan territory.
Dec. 1607	Captain John Smith is captured and taken to Powhatan; he later says that Pocahontas stopped her father from executing him.
May 1608	Powhatan sends Pocahontas to Jamestown to ask for the release of Indian captives.
Oct. 1, 1609	Smith is injured and returns to England, Powhatan is told that Smith is dead.
Nov. 1609	The Powhatans massacre 60 colonists; Pocahontas goes to live with the Patawomekes.
April 1613	Argall kidnaps Pocahontas and brings her to Jamestown.
1614	Pocahontas converts to Christianity and marries John Rolfe; the eight-year Peace of Pocahontas begins.
1615	Pocahontas's son, Thomas, is born.
Spring 1616	Pocahontas goes to England to gain support for the Virginia colony.
March 1617	Pocahontas dies in Gravesend, England.